W9-BHU-400

JOHN COLTRANE
Jazz Revolutionary

JOHN COLTRANE
Jazz Revolutionary

Rachel Stiffler Barron

MORGAN
REYNOLDS
Publishers, Inc.

620 South Elm Street, Suite 223
Greensboro, North Carolina   27406
http://www.morganreynolds.com

JOHN COLTRANE
JAZZ REVOLUTIONARY

Copyright © 2002 by Rachel Stiffler Barron

Cover photograph © Burt and Katherine Holzman Goldblatt

Library of Congress Cataloging-in-Publication Data

Barron, Rachel.
    John Coltrane: Jazz Revolutionary / Rachel Stiffler Barron.
      p. cm.
    Includes bibliographical references (p.) and index.
    Summary: Traces the life of the innovative jazz saxophonist and the evolution of his music.
    ISBN 1-883846-57-9 (lib. bdg.)
      1. Coltrane, John, 1926-1967--Juvenile literature. 2. Jazz musicians--United
    States--Biography--Juvenile literature. [1. Coltrane, John, 1926-1967. 2. Musicians. 3.
    Jazz. 4. African Americans--Biography.] I Title.

    ML3930.C535 B37 2001
      788.7'165'092--dc21
    [B]
                                                              2001010195

Printed in the United States of America
First Edition

To Jim

Contents

John Coltrane, 1960.
(Library of Congress)

Chapter One

A Jazz Genius

In the early 1960s, one of the hottest clubs for jazz in Manhattan was the dark, smoky Half Note at the corner of Spring and Hudson streets. And one of the most popular musicians to pack the house, night after night, was a jazz saxophone player named John Coltrane.

The Half Note had been a restaurant owned by the Canterino family—until their son, Mike Canterino, went off to serve in the navy in Florida. While there, he came to love jazz music, and he was forever changed. He returned home so inspired that he persuaded his whole family to change its restaurant to a jazz club.

It was a smart move for the Canterino family. The club soon gained a reputation for being one of the most off-beat and relaxed jazz clubs in New York. Inside, the windows and walls were painted black, and the lights were kept low. The bandstand was built from Coca-Cola boxes. The Canterinos knocked a large hole in a wall that had once separated the two rooms. No matter which room you sat in, however, you could see only one half of the band at a time.

But that did not seem to bother the devoted fans who came to see John Coltrane and his back-up musicians. He attracted both black and white fans, something quite unusual for the early 1960s.

Most recently, John had made a name for himself as part of trumpeter Miles Davis's group. While with that band, John played saxophone on one of the best-selling jazz albums of all time, *Kind of Blue*. Its success had helped launch his career as a leader of his own band.

John was a pioneer of a new technique of rapid, forceful playing that came to be known as "sheets of sound." Onstage, his energy seemed limitless. He would play for hours, sweating profusely as he poured everything he had into his saxophone. He improvised on a musical phrase, or even a few notes, of a song for long periods of time—sometimes as long as an hour. His music inspired head-nodding and foot-tapping, but it was not easy to dance to. Nevertheless, fans found it fascinating.

The music of John Colrane and Miles Davis had also helped to fuel the flames of a growing racial unrest and burgeoning civil rights movement. Unlike black musicians of generations before, Miles had refused to pander to white audiences' tastes. He played the music he wanted to play, even turning his back on the audience at times. White fans liked the music, but black followers were also inspired by something else: his strong will and willingness to buck popular culture.

In some ways, John was now carrying on Miles's legacy with his free-form playing. As Mike Canterino later said, "We seemed to attract the most politically advanced blacks whenever Trane was appearing. He'd take a long solo, probably close to an hour, and these guys would be shouting 'Freedom now!' all over the place. It was like they were using his music as a rallying cry for whatever political movements they were into."

Some even considered it a spiritual experience, for John Coltrane played the saxophone in an almost superhuman way. John himself was a deeply spiritual man. Between sets, he sat in the kitchen, eating pizza and reading the Bible.

Not everyone, however, loved John's music. Throughout his career, he had many critics and detractors. As he evolved spiritually and musically, his playing would become so unusual that even some of his most devoted fans would not make the journey with him. Some would boo him and walk out on his performances. But John Coltrane would follow his heart to the end, always true to himself and his music.

John Coltrane was born in the small town of Hamlet, North Carolina. Although John and his family were black, the name Coltrane, as well as his mother's maiden name of Blair, were both Scottish. Two hundred years before, black families had been brought to the area as slaves, and most were named after their white owners.

John's mother, Alice Blair Coltrane, was the seventh of eight children born to the Reverend William Blair, an African Methodist Episcopal (AME) Zion minister, and his wife, also named Alice. All of the Blairs were literate, which was unusual among blacks of the late 1800s. The Reverend Blair had an extensive library of religious books as well as books of black American history and works of black poets.

The family had lived in Edenton, North Carolina, but while Alice was still young, they moved to Tampa, Florida, for a time. The move apparently took place because the Reverend Blair had been active in politics with the Republican Party, which in those days courted black support. This did not sit well with the Ku Klux Klan, a white supremacist group that committed violent acts to terrorize blacks. One night members of the Klan rode through the Blairs' yard in Edenton on their horses, sending a clear, threatening message. The family abruptly left the area and moved to Tampa.

By 1920, though, the Blairs were back in North Carolina, this time in High Point, a city now known internationally for furniture manufacturing. Alice enrolled at Livingstone College, a black college affiliated with the AME Zion church in nearby Salisbury. She was a fine singer and played the piano for the Reverend Blair's church choir on Sundays.

After she graduated in 1925, Alice moved to Hamlet to marry a young tailor named John Robert "J. R." Coltrane, also the son of an AME Zion minister. Her new husband also loved music and could play the violin and the ukulele. The newly married couple lived in a second-floor apartment of a boarding house in Hamlet. J. R. worked as a tailor and pressed clothes.

It was not long before their young marriage suffered

its first tragedy when their first child died in infancy. Alice soon became pregnant again, however, and she and her husband rejoiced when their son John was born at home the afternoon of September 23, 1926.

Within a few months after John's birth, the family moved back to High Point to live with Alice's father. The elder Reverend Blair had retired as a full-time minister and was now serving as a bishop. Although he traveled, visiting churches in southeastern North Carolina, Reverend Blair was still the dominating presence in the family.

His family's religious faith had a profound influence on John's life. John said:

> My mother, she was very religious. Like, in my early years I was going to church every Sunday and stuff like that, being under the influence of my grandfather—he was the dominating cat in the family. He was most well versed, active politically. He was more active than my father, [who] was a tailor; but he [Coltrane's father] never seemed to say too much. He just went about his business, and that was it. But my grandfather, he was pretty militant, you know. Politically inclined and everything.

At the time, High Point was a growing town of about 35,000 citizens, a third of whom were black. The city had two all-black neighborhoods. The poorer neighborhood was on the southside. Three miles away, the more affluent black families lived on the eastside, only one street over from where the wealthy whites lived.

The Reverend Blair's house was in the center of the eastside, a two-story frame house with an open porch, an adjoining carport and driveway. The street in front of the house was paved, which indicated that the family was well off financially. Reverend Blair was also one of a minority of blacks who owned a home.

The first story of the house had a large living room, dining room, small bathroom, and country-style kitchen. The upstairs had three bedrooms and a bathroom with a large four-footed tub. Including the elderly Blairs, the Coltrane family of three, and other family members, eight people lived in the house. Children and their parents slept in the same room.

Even as a young child, John was a quiet, private person. He became close to his cousin Mary, who also lived with the family. John and Mary came to regard each other as brother and sister instead of cousins. John was always shy and reluctant to talk about himself, even after he became famous. Much of what we know about him now comes from his cousin Mary.

John and Mary made many friends in the neighborhood. Life was simple; Saturdays were for going to Shirley Temple movies and roller-skating. Mary later described John as "basically a good child, but he was mischievous and he always had this dry sense of humor. Basically he was very quiet."

Another friend, Betty Jackson, said John was "a very neat child. All of his work was neat; all of his papers

John Coltrane grew up in High Point, NC. He is pictured here (third row, second from left) with his classmates at Leonard Street School in 1934. *(High Point Museum)*

were exact." Although John joined in rough and tumble games with other boys, he always had a dignity that set him apart, Betty said. "Their [other boys'] socks would be one up and one down, but he was always neat."

John's family was close to the family of another one of his friends, Betty Leach. The two families ate dinner together every Monday night. "We'd have hominy grits, rice, oatmeal, fried chicken, corn bread, collard greens— and my favorite, sweet potato pie," she said.

John's father loved to invite friends to the house in the evenings, where they would sit around and talk, laugh, and play music. Often J. R. would play his favorite song, "The Sweetheart of Sigma Chi," on the ukulele. John, who by this time had large, luminous eyes, watched quietly. The song, a waltz, became a personal favorite, too. Years later he would record it himself.

But in late 1938, the happy times suddenly gave way to tragedy for twelve-year-old John Coltrane.

First an elderly aunt who lived in Virginia passed away. John and Mary were spared from journeying to that funeral, but shortly afterward, on December 11, 1938, seventy-nine-year-old Reverend Blair, the pillar of the family, passed away after becoming ill with pneumonia.

There was no way for the family to shelter John and Mary from this tragedy. Their grandfather's body was displayed in their home for friends and relatives to visit before the funeral. "I had never seen anything like that before," Mary said. "Only one time before that had I been to a funeral, and that upset me."

John and Mary did not know it at the time, but another tragedy was about to strike. In November, John's father had been diagnosed with stomach cancer. The adults in the family kept this to themselves, so it came as a terrible shock to John and Mary when, less than a month after their grandfather's death, J. R. Coltrane went to the hospital. He died there a few days later.

At that time, stomach cancer was the most common kind of cancer. Many years later, researchers discovered that it is linked to poor diet: high salt, low fiber, low protein—and food that is not completely fresh. Although more attention to diet and good refrigeration has reduced stomach cancer in the United States, even today it is a silent disease that often does not show symptoms until it is too late to be successfully treated.

Finally, just three months later, the Reverend Blair's widow Alice—John and Mary's grandmother—died of breast cancer. Mary knew that her grandmother had a lump in her breast, and she had actually ridden with her in a taxicab to the hospital a number of times for radiation treatment. But, characteristic of the way the family dealt with illnesses privately, the word "cancer" was never spoken out loud. It was not until many years later that John and Mary understood the cause of their grandmother's death.

The deaths were devastating to the children. As Mary would later say, "We had them all that time and then all of a sudden they were all gone, with only months in between. John couldn't even remember what his father looked like. He would say to me, 'Mary, what did Daddy look like?' I would talk to him and I would tell him what he looked like."

Unfortunately, this was not the end of the family's troubles. Mary's father and John's uncle, Goler Lyerly, moved into the home and served as the father figure for a time. But a year later, due to chronic asthma and an enlarged heart, he, too, passed away.

The deaths had a profound impact on the family. Without any men living in the home, Mary, John, and their mothers now found themselves scrambling to make ends meet. "Our mothers had to go to work, and my aunt and my mother worked together at a country club," Mary said. "John used to shine shoes there. We had to rent out our bedrooms and we all slept downstairs. My mother, John and I all slept in the dining room. John's mother slept upstairs in the bedroom because she had arthritis and needed special attention. We had cots." John was sick much of the time with something similar to asthma, Mary added, and "we had to sit up with him at night. This went on for a long time."

High Point's black community was warm and supportive, and friends and neighbors regularly pitched in to help the family. But it was a time of segregation throughout the South, and outside of their communities blacks in High Point were second-class citizens. While there was no violence, whites and blacks lived very separate lives in their own neighborhoods and schools.

"If the white schools got new books one year, the blacks might have got them a few years later," said Rufus Leach Jr., a friend of Coltrane's in High Point. "They [black schools] got used books from the white schools. But nobody spoke up at that time—even the principal had to go along with it."

Both white and black schools taught trades such as bricklaying and carpentry, but students learned on different equipment. "We had about three little machines down there [at the black school]," Leach said. "One day I went down to the white high school. It looked like a factory, with all the machinery lined up and down on both sides. If one didn't work right, they'd probably give it to us!"

But John had discovered a pastime that took his mind off all of these troubles. Not long after his father's death, he and several friends learned to play wind instruments in a community band led by Warren B. Steele. The boys had first met Steele because he was the leader of their Boy Scout troop. Steele was not a formally trained music teacher, but he was smart and talented and had played in military bands during World War I. The band had no money, so Steele borrowed some instruments and scraped up others anywhere he could find them, often from pawnshops.

Steele started young John Coltrane on the alto horn, a smaller relative of the tuba. But one day a clarinet player did not show up for practice, and John asked Steele if he could just hold the boy's instrument for a few minutes. While Steele watched, John put the clarinet's mouthpiece in his mouth and blew a few notes that came out unusually clear and melodic for a beginner.

Steele was surprised—and curious. "Have you been learning on the side? Watching somebody else playing?" he asked John.

"Well, maybe watching you teach the other clarinet players, Reverend Steele," John replied modestly.

The next week at band practice, the clarinet section had a new member, John Coltrane. Steele had just "happened to find another clarinet lying around" and gave it to John.

Although the little band played only simple marching tunes, and each member only knew one or two songs, it was promising enough to inspire the principal at William Penn High School to start a school band. The PTA managed to raise enough money through socials, teas, and rummage sales to buy six clarinets and a set of drums. John and his friends from the community band became the founding members of the new high school band. None of the students owned their own instruments; they remained the property of the school.

The high school band was fortunate to have a talented young black woman as a teacher, Grace Yokely, who had studied with Dr. Nathaniel Dett, a noted composer. Yokely was very impressed that John was talented enough to pick out popular tunes on the clarinet just by listening to recordings of the big bands. "I remember John being a very fine little boy, a very conscientious type child," Yokely told a reporter years later, after John had become famous. "He showed great interest in wanting to get everything just right. He was a very rhythmic fellow, and he paid attention."

In the fall of 1940, when John was fourteen, he became interested in the saxophone. Lester Young, who had become well-known as the tenor saxophonist in the Count Basie Orchestra, was his new idol. Young was famous for his light, brisk tone and finely crafted, improvised (made-up) solos.

John started out on a borrowed alto saxophone. He improved quickly because he practiced so much. Mary later remembered his practicing habits: "He would sit at the [dining room] table and practice all the time. He practiced *all* the time."

John had apparently turned to music as a way to deal with his grief. During his family's tragedies, John had quietly kept his feelings bottled inside. Although he

Lester Young, a famous saxophonist in the Count Basie Orchestra, inspired Coltrane to begin playing the saxophone himself. *(Library of Congress)*

outwardly appeared calm and unruffled, he poured his energy into practicing. David Young, one of John's high school friends, said, "For a while, I don't think he had anything but that horn." As he focused more heavily on his music, John's grades slipped. While he had previously been an A student, he now earned many Cs.

When he was not rehearsing, John listened to music on the radio. Although white station managers played little music by black artists, favorites by such big band leaders as Duke Ellington and Count Basie, and trumpeter Louis Armstrong, did get some airplay. John and Mary also attended concerts at a nearby theater when swing bands came to town, although they and other blacks had to sit high up in the balcony, far away from the stage, while white patrons enjoyed the good seats.

When John became a senior in high school, his mother, Alice, moved to Atlantic City, New Jersey, where opportunities for African Americans were better than in the South. John and his mother were very close, and her departure made him lonelier than ever. But he was becoming quite popular with his classmates. His musical talent and loner personality, along with some nice clothes he had bought with his earnings from a part-time job in a soda shop, gave him a mystique that interested girls.

The racial segregation of High Point was something John would never forget, however. During his senior year of high school, he came to resent the fact that the football team on which he played had substandard equipment and ragged uniforms that did not match.

Shortly after his graduation, John headed north. Some of his friends had moved to Philadelphia, and John followed, hoping for a less segregated environment and more opportunities to expand his musical talents.

After he left, John rarely visited High Point or even mentioned that he had grown up there. "He didn't like to go down [South] and play because he didn't like playing for a segregated audience," Mary said. While other black musicians would tolerate the segregation and go out on the black side of town to enjoy themselves after playing a concert in a Southern city, John would return to his hotel room to spend a quiet evening alone.

Chapter Two

A Young Man in the Big City

The city of Philadelphia was a far different place from High Point, North Carolina. There were many more social activities and no Jim Crow laws. When he moved there in June 1943, John lived closer to his mother in New Jersey. She bought him an alto saxophone—the first instrument he ever owned.

But now John and his friends were presented with a new problem. World War II was in full swing, and they faced the likelihood of being drafted. This made it difficult to make any long-term plans, either for work or college.

At age seventeen, John was a year younger than most of his friends in Philadelphia. He would be eligible for the draft when he turned eighteen. While they waited to see if this would happen, they did their best to enjoy the city. Their favorite activity was going to nightclubs to listen to and play music.

John and his other musician friends were about to be swept up in a musical revolution. The "big bands," led by Duke Ellington, Tommy Dorsey, Benny Goodman and others, had reigned over the music world since the 1920s. They played boisterous dance music that cheered audiences through the grimmest days of the war. But now they were declining because so many of their members had been drafted to fight the war. This left room for a new form of jazz music, one that could be played by smaller groups, to emerge.

It is generally agreed that jazz had its origin in New Orleans, Louisiana, around the turn of the century. Just as rock and rap music would be decades later, the new jazz music was feared as the downfall of America's youth and moral character by many adults. It was music played in smoky, dark nightclubs. As early as the 1920s, some of these dance halls looked the other way while blacks and whites mingled in the audience and even danced together—something that occurred nowhere else in American society. Jazz was a symbol of modernism, excitement, and rebellion.

But jazz represented something deeper as well. It was a unique expression of democracy, of the American spirit. Musicians might start off playing from an established melody or series of chords. Then, in their improvised solos, the players allowed the feeling and emotion of the moment to carry them off into new directions that altered the original structure of the song. As they played in groups, musicians often used their solos to "talk" to one another. One might play a solo for a few minutes, then be "answered" by another who took his turn. Jazz held a special attraction for African Americans, because it inspired a feeling of freedom and openness they were not normally allowed to display in everyday life.

One of the early jazz pioneers was Duke Ellington, one of the first African-Americans to succeed in music among both blacks and whites. In addition to leading his own orchestra, "The Duke" wrote nearly 2,000 pieces of big band music. Another important figure was trumpet player Louis Armstrong, the first musician to get out front and play lengthy solos while other members of the big band backed him up.

In the 1940s, a new form of jazz was emerging in which the musicians felt even more free to depart from their sheet music. They added, substituted, and deleted chords to the point that sometimes audiences could no longer recognize the underlying melody of the song they were playing. This new form of music that had been dubbed "bebop," or simply "bop," required a higher level of musicianship than the earlier big band or "swing" music. To play bop, the instrumentalist had to know the chord structure of the piece, and also had to know how to alter the underlying chords in a way that both made sense and that created a new melody. All this happened instantaneously, as he or she was playing a solo.

The new music was often, especially at first hearing, less melodious than the earlier styles of jazz. It was less concerned with pleasing the casual listener and more intent on impressing audiences with the originality of the soloist's improvisational skill. It was also controversial. Louis Armstrong called it "Chinese music" because of its different harmonic structure. Many older swing players spoke out against it, and radio stations did not want to play it. But there was no stopping this new, "modern" jazz. It grew in popularity through exposure in nightclubs and back rooms.

Next door to John's apartment was a club that was popular with local musicians. Famous musicians, such as Ellington, occasionally dropped by to jam after they finished their gigs at other clubs. The action went on into the wee hours of the morning. John and his friends spent many evenings there.

During the daytime, John worked in a sugar-refining factory and took classes at the Ornstein School of Music. The school was one of the most prestigious in Philadelphia. His teacher there was Mike Guerra who, like Coltrane, had switched from clarinet to saxophone.

John was delighted when his cousin Mary also moved to Philadelphia after graduating from high school. Mary was happy to live near John again, despite his constant practicing. "We never looked at John as a genius. He was [just] John," Mary said later. "We all just lived in those two rooms, and he would just sit there all the time and practice and smoke cigarettes. He would sit at my vanity and look at himself in the mirror playing his horn. We were used to his practicing, but the neighbors were not. When they complained, the minister of the church we attended gave John a key to the church. He could go there anytime he wanted and practice."

One of John's idols was Johnny Hodges, an alto saxophonist in Duke Ellington's band. John spent many hours imitating Hodges's sound on his own alto sax. This greatly impressed his friends, who began joking that Coltrane was "the next Johnny Hodges." One of his friends, Benny Golson, who was also a talented saxophonist, later recalled that his mother was so taken with John's rendition of "On the Sunny Side of the Street," a tune for which Hodges was famous, that she demanded John play it for her every time he came over. John was fond of romantic ballads in general, perhaps because his father had loved them as well.

One evening John and Benny went to see Dizzy Gillespie, one of the pioneers of bebop, in concert at a theater in Philadelphia. They were sitting in the cheapest seats at the back of the balcony. When the band took a break, a "short, squat guy in a pinstripe suit stepped on stage," Benny remembered. "He started playing alto while coming out of a crouch. John just sat there, taking it all in. All over the hall, people were standing up and shouting, clapping their hands and stamping their feet. Imagine being a saxophonist and never having heard this kind of music before." The saxophonist was Charlie "Bird" Parker, one of the founders of bop.

After the show Benny and John went backstage to get Parker's autograph. While Benny walked right up to get in the autograph line, John stood in awe off in the corner, shyly watching Parker talk to his fans. Although only six years older than John, Parker was far more self-confident and outgoing. When he noticed John staring quietly in the corner he joked, "Well, young man, you are not a chicken, so I'm not going to eat you, and you are not a saxophone, so I'm not going to play you. Exactly what is it you want?" Then, realizing how shy John was, he put his arm around John's shoulders and asked, "Do you play, my fine young fellow?"

Benny, knowing that John would be too modest, spoke up: "He plays alto... And I think he plays it very well."

"And who might you be, his older brother?" Parker joked to Benny.

Benny and John explained that they were simply friends and fellow musicians out enjoying a concert. "Well, the next time I visit Philadelphia I would like to hear you play," Parker said to them. Before he turned to leave, he asked John, "And just what name do you go under, my man?"

John replied, "John Coltrane." Parker asked him to repeat it, then to spell it. Finally, he said, "I like your name, my man. It reminds of a quality brand of English muffins."

John's musical education ended temporarily when he was finally drafted. Fortunately, World War II was nearly over by this time. In fact, the day he joined—August 6, 1945—was the same day that the United States dropped the first atomic bomb on Japan.

After finishing boot camp, John was assigned to the Ha-

Coltrane worked to imitate his idol Johnny Hodges, an alto saxophonist in Duke Ellington's band. *(Library of Congress)*

waiian island of Oahu to play in a navy swing band known as the Melody Masters. Like many young black men of the time, John did not care for military life. Although fighting to liberate the European and Asian countries that had been overrun by the Nazis and Japanese was an honorable cause, the war was a bitter experience for many African Americans. While they were expected to sacrifice their lives if necessary to fight oppression overseas, rampant racism was an accepted way of life in the military.

Just like American society, the navy was segregated, with separate housing and cafeterias for whites and blacks. Even blood supplies donated by black and white soldiers were kept separate. Members of white navy bands had much free time when they were not playing, but members of black bands had other obligations such as kitchen duty. In fact, blacks were not even considered official members of the U.S. Navy, but of the U.S. Naval Reserves. Even German prisoners of war who had been captured were allowed to eat in the "white" cafeterias on U.S. bases, while the blacks had to eat in a separate area.

Fortunately, military musicians did not observe racial barriers. Although they could not perform together in public, it was common for white seamen to sneak over to the "black side" of the island at night—or vice versa—for jam sessions. They even recorded these integrated sessions and had a few 78s—large vinyl records—pressed of the performances.

A few of these recordings still exist today. Although

One of the most famous saxophonists ever, Charlie "Bird" Parker helped to found the "bop" style of music that Coltrane enjoyed playing. *(Library of Congress)*

John sounds promising on these old recordings, he still had a great deal to learn. It would only be after years of hard work, long hours of practice and jamming with other musicians before he found his distinctive voice.

John spent only a year in the navy. The war had ended and the bands were no longer necessary to keep up morale for the soldiers. He headed back to Philadelphia, more determined than ever to pursue his musical interests. And, thanks to the military, he could now qualify for veterans' housing loans and free tuition to college under the GI Bill.

Coltrane used those benefits to pay his tuition for a music school in Philadelphia. Isadore Granoff, the Russian immigrant who founded the school, believed strongly that jazz musicians should receive traditional classical training. This was contrary to the way most jazz musicians learned to play. Most were self-taught or learned from jamming with more accomplished players. Granoff insisted that the jazz musicians read sheet music and learn the fundamentals of theory, harmony, and ear training.

John's most influential teacher at the Granoff School was Dennis Sandole, who was impressed by John's dedication and enthusiasm. His method of teaching was complex and incorporated ethnic influences and exotic scales from around the world. He also persuaded John to listen to classical music by European composers such as Debussy, Ravel, and Bartók. Sandole's influence helped to make John more receptive to new ideas and influences. This would have a profound impact on his music.

The GI Bill paid for all of his classes, books, and supplies—as well as an allowance of $65 a month. In exchange, John was required to attend classes or lessons for twenty-five hours a week. A typical student only took one or two lessons per week. This did not bother John, who was used to long hours of practicing. In fact, he frequently sat up long into the night practicing his fingering without blowing into the horn so as to not disturb his neighbors.

John's schooling was interrupted from time to time when he found work with a traveling band. One job was with Eddie "Cleanhead" Vinson, a band leader and alto saxophonist. As he passed through Philadelphia in 1947, he came across John playing in a club. Vinson immediately wanted to hire him, but there was one problem. Because Vinson played the alto saxophone himself, he did not need another alto saxophonist. He offered John a job playing tenor sax instead.

John balked at first. Finally, Vinson said, "Look, Johnny, I'll buy you a tenor and you can jam on alto after hours, 'cause there's always places where you can do that. Now, what do you say?" John agreed, deciding that traveling in Vinson's band would be a good experience even if he had to play tenor.

Playing tenor sax was an adjustment for John. It was bigger, heavier, and required much more of his energy to blow air through it effectively. But he slowly grew to love it. He and Vinson played well together and even developed an entertaining routine in which one of them would play a line, then quickly exchange horns with the other man, who would repeat it note for note, then toss it back. In addition to being a crowd-pleaser, this was a good exercise in coordination. Vinson's music, though, was not as challenging as the new modern jazz, and soon John grew bored with playing the same riffs night after night.

John also did not like the traveling band life. He was homesick for his family and friends. He had also developed bad eating habits. He had always had a sweet tooth, and while traveling he ate candy bars and drank soft drinks more than ever. The high sugar consumption was damaging his teeth and he began to have painful toothaches, but he was terrified of going to dentists. Playing the saxophone made his toothaches more excruciating and he began drinking heavily to dull the pain. He was also smoking heavily. Finally Vinson insisted that John go to a dentist, who pulled two of his teeth that had decayed beyond repair.

The jazz world had plenty of bad influences, including Vinson, whose own heavy drinking and erratic personality eventually led to the break-up of the band. He and many other musicians of the day had been influenced by Charlie Parker, who was a heroin addict. Many young musicians mistakenly believed that heroin made Parker a better saxophonist, so they tried it, too, and soon many talented musicians were addicts.

Parker eventually made a public statement that heroin did *not* improve his music, but by then it was too late. Many lost control of their lives, borrowing money or stealing to support their habit. Others went to prison, thanks to the tough drug laws. Eventually, Parker and a number of other famous musicians died from the ravages of addiction.

John fell victim to the plague and became a heroin addict. Because he was a quiet, withdrawn drug user who drew little attention to himself, he managed to avoid trouble with the law. But his addictions to alcohol and heroin tarnished his image and limited his potential in the coming years.

Chapter Three

Touring with Dizzy

In September 1949, a few months after he left Vinson's band, John landed a spot in a big band led by Dizzy Gillespie. Although Gillespie had been one of the founders of bop, the music that hastened the decline in popularity of big bands, he wanted to try out some of the new ideas with a larger group. Dizzy enjoyed arranging for an orchestra and wanted to try out some of the new musical ideas that had been worked out with small combos in the larger setting.

Gillespie was a controversial figure. Although he avoided becoming addicted and was one of the theoreticians of modern jazz, he did have a hot temper. He spoke out against segregation and was at the forefront of a new generation who rejected the subservient role often played by black artists of the past. In fact, bebop music in general was seen as a reflection of the anger and frustration he and other black musicians felt.

After John joined, the band began a national tour beginning at the Earle Theatre in Philadelphia, a venue that most young musicians could only dream of playing.

Franklin Brower, one of John's friends from High Point, was also living in Philadelphia and writing for the *Philadelphia Afro-American*. He devoted a column to the twenty-three-year-old saxophonist from North Carolina who was realizing his dream of playing in a first-rate band. This was the first article written about Coltrane.

While playing with Dizzy, John met Yusef Lateef, a tenor saxophonist and orthodox Muslim. A large, imposing bald man nicknamed the "Gentle Giant," Lateef persuaded John to read the writings of the Arab American philosopher and poet Kahlil Gibran and Jiddu Kristnamurti, a spiritual leader from India. John also read the Koran, the sacred book of the Islamic faith. Another musician, Bill Barron, gave him a book on yoga. These influences from Eastern religion were very different from what John had grown up with in the AME Zion church, and they encouraged him on his lifelong spiritual journey.

John enjoyed the fellowship of playing with Dizzy Gillespie and his musicians, but there were some frustrations. By now he had actually come to prefer playing tenor sax, but in Dizzy's band he had to play alto. And there was the constant traveling, particularly in the racially tense southern states. One day, the band stopped at a gas station and café outside the little town of Mexico, Missouri. The band members were ravenously hungry, but they were greeted by the white café manager with just four words: "We don't serve niggers."

The band's mix of traditional jazz and bebop caused

problems with both the players and audiences. Gillespie wanted to continue playing bop, but he also wanted the music to be danceable and popular with his audiences. This led to an odd mix of music that did not quite satisfy anyone. But the experience was a valuable one for John as a musician. Gillespie was by this time intrigued with Latin music, and the fusion of his new interest with jazz inspired Coltrane to continue studying the music of other cultures and to incorporate them into his own playing.

Gillespie was a good mentor to the younger players. Jimmy Heath, another band member, described him this way: "Dizzy was a great teacher and giver. He was the most accessible genius I've ever known."

It soon became too difficult to keep a sixteen piece band on the road, however. Financial pressures forced Gillespie to form a smaller band for touring. He kept John as the sole tenor saxophonist.

John's career was taking off. He was improving as a musician. But he was still using heroin and drinking heavily. Gillespie discovered that several members of the band, including John, had become addicted to drugs. While in Los Angeles in late 1950, John fell unconscious in his hotel room, and Jimmy Heath revived him. This frightened Coltrane enough to quit heroin for a time, but he continued drinking heavily.

Gillespie, who hated the toll that drugs and alcohol were taking on jazz musicians, lost his patience and fired several band members, including John. The others were too proud to ask for another chance, but John

Dizzy Gillespie, a talented and controversial figure in jazz, offered Coltrane a spot in his popular jazz band. *(Library of Congress)*

begged to stay on, and Gillespie relented. But by April 1951, Coltrane was no longer playing with Gillespie. He was still drinking and had returned to heroin.

Billy Taylor, a pianist with the band, said of John:

> He was a very soft spoken and nice guy. It was frustrating for me because he was one of the first people that I met that I said, 'Gee, I wish there was something I could say or something I could do to convince him not to do this.' And I didn't know him that well and I didn't want to impose—it wouldn't do any good. I said some things, but nothing that would change his mind at that time.

For the next few years, John played in less familiar bands and continued taking lessons and practicing. During 1952 he played with a band led by alto saxophonist Earl Bostic, who was respected for his technical mastery of his instrument, although he was more of a rhythm and blues player than a jazz artist. John took every opportunity to learn from Bostic. As they drove in the car between gigs, he would pepper his boss with questions about playing the sax and write down his replies in a notebook.

Despite his addictions, John tried his best to lead an honorable life. He now had enough money to move his family to a larger house. He and Mary, his mother, Alice, and his friend James Kinzer had outgrown their space in the apartment building. John used his veteran's benefits to get a low-interest loan for a house on what had been the exclusively white North 23rd Street. This new house provided more room for his mother's upright piano and for jam sessions and rehearsals.

In 1954, John realized a special dream when he was invited to play in a band led by his idol, Johnny Hodges. But John's drug problems soon began to interfere with his work in this band, too. Sometimes he would nod off while waiting for his solo, and one of his fellow band members would nudge him awake so that Hodges did not notice.

Finally Coltrane's behavior became too noticeable for Hodges to ignore. John Williams, who played bass in the band, explained:

> Coltrane would be sitting in his chair, holding his horn but not moving his fingers, the sax still in his mouth but not playing. It was obvious that he was using drugs, and when this got to be a habit, Hodges talked to him and asked him to watch it. John agreed with him, realizing Johnny [Hodges] was right. But the next night, or the night after that, it would happen all over again, just as before.

With the overeating, heavy drinking, and heroin use, John's weight ballooned. His teeth continued to bother him, too. All of these things took their toll on John and forced him to think more about his life. He wondered where he was going musically and why he had ever gotten started on drugs and alcohol.

Fortunately for John, at that time he met someone who would help him change his life for the better. She had been born Juanita Austin in North Carolina but was now living in Philadelphia with her mother and her young daughter, Syeeda. She had become a devout Muslim and changed her name to Naima.

At the time, converting to the Muslim faith appealed to many young blacks who felt that Christianity was dominated by whites who had never really accepted them as equals. Ironically, society seemed to support this bias. Many stores and restaurants that would not serve "coloreds" would serve "Muslims," so this provided something of an escape from racial discrimination.

Naima was grounded and sensible, and her influence helped John begin to dig his way out of his years of addiction. She also loved music and could have long conversations with John about it. Although John was not a member of any organized religion, Naima realized that he was a very spiritual person.

After only a few months of dating, John announced that he was serious about Naima. They were sharing a hoagie sandwich in a restaurant when he said, very matter-of-factly, that he was going to marry her.

"How do you know that?" she exclaimed. "You haven't even asked me!"

"Then I'll ask you now," he said. He quietly proposed to her, right there in the restaurant.

They were married on October 3, 1955. Naima and Syeeda moved in with John's family on North 23rd Street.

Things began improving for John's career as well. He was invited to join a band led by an already legend-

In 1955, John married his first wife, Naima, and began to play with jazz great Miles Davis. *(© Burt and Katherine Holzman Goldblatt)*

ary musician named Miles Davis. Davis was the same age as John and had grown up in St. Louis, which had its own thriving jazz culture. Big bands touring through St. Louis, struggling to find good players during the war years, offered him jobs while he was still a teenager.

After graduating from high school, Davis moved to New York, where he became part of the jazz scene. While he was influenced by what he heard around him—and did an extended stint playing with Charlie Parker—Davis was very much an individual. By the late 1940s he had decided that bop had developed as far as it could go. Most bop tunes were driven by the chords, which meant the soloist was locked into a system of adapting the underlying chord changes. The arrangements of the small bop combos were also usually simple—an introduction, successive solos, then an ensemble finish. Davis, who was never a great player at the higher registers and did not have the huge sound of Dizzy Gillespie, became the leader of a nine-man band that played slower, quieter music often arranged with more interplay of the instruments. He took the band into the studio and cut a highly influential album that was later released with the title *The Birth of the Cool*, because the tunes were played at a more moderate tempo than the blazing fast bop style. Davis would forever be identified with this new sound, which was dubbed "cool jazz." While Davis was never able to blow the roof down like Louis Armstrong or Dizzy, his trumpet playing had a beautiful, lyrical sound accented by his use of a Harmon mute, a metal mute placed on the end of a trumpet. Davis usually played in a minimalist style. He looked for the absolute right note instead of trying to come up with an overwhelming stream of sounds. The term "cool" also reflected the way he hardly seemed to care if the audience liked him or not. Sometimes he even played long stretches with his back turned to the audience.

Davis's career had dipped while he had his own struggles with heroin. He was able to kick his habit in the early 1950s and begin slowly rebuilding his career. He was a huge hit at the Newport Jazz Festival in July 1955 and was beginning to refine his distinct sound in recordings. All eyes were on Miles Davis and there was

a great deal of interest in the new quintet he put together. When he selected John Coltrane as the tenor
saxophonist, John suddenly acquired a nickname—
"Trane"—that would soon become famous all over the
world.

Chapter Four

Touring with Miles and Monk

Playing with Miles Davis presented John with some new and tough challenges. Although he was making rapid development, John was still forming his own style as a tenor saxophonist. It was becoming obvious that his style was unusual. One of the techniques he was developing was to borrow riffs for his solos from music of other cultures, such as India. But many people did not understand what he was doing. They took this experimenting for bad saxophone playing. Music critics who wrote for newspapers and magazines were sharply divided about John Coltrane. Some thought his playing was not really jazz; others recognized that he had something unique to say, if the listener would only be open-minded and patient.

There was also some tension between John and Miles. Years later, Miles wrote in his autobiography about their relationship: "Trane liked to ask all these questions back then about what he should or shouldn't play. To me he was a professional musician and I have always wanted whoever played with me to find their own place in the music. So my silence and evil looks probably turned him off."

John told an interviewer:

> Miles is a strange guy. He doesn't talk much and he rarely discusses music. You always have the impression that he's in a bad mood, and that what concerns others doesn't interest him or move him. Miles's reactions are completely unpredictable. He'll play with us for a few measures, then—you never know when—he'll leave us on our own. And if you ask him something about music, you never know how he's going to take it. You always have to listen carefully to stay in the same mood as he!

By taking the spot in Miles's band, John had replaced Sonny Rollins, a popular musician who had decided to take a year off from performing to kick his heroin habit. Some audience members would show up to a performance expecting to hear Sonny and were disappointed to hear the relatively unknown John Coltrane instead.

Sy Johnson, a composer and pianist who heard the band frequently, said that the Miles Davis band "blew everybody out of the water . . . (but) I had to convince people to listen to Coltrane. They would say, 'When that tenor player plays I just tune him out and listen to the bass player.' One problem was that everybody was sure the tenor player was going to be Sonny Rollins."

None of this controversy helped John with the lack

of self-confidence that plagued him. He knew it was a great honor to have been picked for the band, but in some ways he felt he did not deserve it. He was full of guilt about his drug use and how it had retarded his career. "All the things I started to do in 1955, when I went with him [Miles], were some of the things I felt I should have done in '47 and '48," he said later.

On another occasion, he said:

> When I first joined Miles in 1955 I had a lot to learn. I felt I was lacking in general musician-ship. I had all kinds of technical problems—for example, I didn't have the right mouth-piece—and I hadn't the necessary harmonic understanding. Why he picked me, I don't know. Maybe he saw something in my play-ing that he hoped would grow. I had this desire, which I think we all have, to be as original as I could, and as honest as I could be. But there were so many musical conclusions I hadn't arrived at, that I felt inadequate. All this was naturally frustrating in those days, and it came through in the music.

In fact, many people told Miles that he should get rid of John and drummer Philly Joe Jones, another contro-versial member of the band. But Miles stuck by them both. "People used to tell me Trane couldn't play and Philly Joe played too loud," Miles said later. "But I know what I want, and if I didn't think they knew what they were doing, they wouldn't be there."

Miles Davis, one of the greatest jazz legends of all time, chose John Coltrane to play saxaphone in his band. *(Library of Congress)*

Some musicians who found John thoroughly likable on a personal level had a difficult time understanding his music. But John was open to discussing music with anyone who would listen, and many found that if they took the time to talk with him, they gained a new appreciation of his style.

David Amram, who encountered John eating a piece of pie on a sidewalk during an intermission, said: "I remember his eyes, huge but not staring, friendly and almost bemused. We looked at each other for the longest time, until I said hello and told him how much I liked his music."

The two men stood there for a few minutes, talking. John told David that he "was trying to make music beyond the 32-bar song form, to constantly develop and improvise on an idea or a simple line, as Indian musicians do with a raga. I think this was the most serious musical discussion during the shortest amount of time I've ever had in my life."

Slowly, John began to establish his reputation and to win respect. When Columbia Records, a major recording label, lured the Miles Davis Quintet away from the smaller Prestige Records with a more lucrative contract, John Coltrane came along as part of the package.

George Avakian, the producer who had recruited the Miles Davis Quintet to come to Columbia, described the way he felt when he first met John:

> He reminded me of a large cherub, though a rather expressionless one. He was not easy to

start a conversation with, but I sensed the depths of the man and I felt he was highly intelligent. Our family is Armenian, and when I mentioned my interest in Eastern cultures, John really opened up. He told me about books he'd read and things he'd learned that were well in advance of my personal knowledge at that time. While we talked, I couldn't help noticing his eyes. They had an arresting quality, and whenever he looked at me, or anyone else, he really looked deeply.

The band's first album for Columbia was called *Round about Midnight*. The album was a success, and John was beginning to develop a following. He moved his family from Philadelphia to New York City, where he could be closer to the record producers and recording studios.

But John's bad habits continued to plague him. He was still using heroin. Whenever he tried to quit, he drank alcohol to get through the withdrawal. It was a vicious cycle that was taking a toll on his health.

Ira Gitler, a jazz writer who saw the Miles Davis group play at the Café Bohemia in Greenwich Village a number of times, noticed that John routinely disappeared during breaks in the sets. "He would be in the basement practicing, and he was drinking a mixture of wine and beer. I guess he was trying to kick heroin. He just wasn't too communicative."

Miles had kicked his own heroin habit, so he had little patience for John's—or any other musician's—

drug use. He cared only about the music, and John's addiction was hurting his performance. He appeared to be nodding off on stage when he was not playing and he was neglecting his personal hygiene. "He'd be playing in clothes that looked like he had slept in them for days, all wrinkled up and dirty," Miles said.

After giving John several warnings to kick his drug habit, Miles finally fired him in 1957. "Man, it was a drag to see how bad Trane was treating himself," Miles wrote in his own autobiography. "One night I got so mad with him that I slapped him upside his head and punched him in the stomach in the dressing room . . . I felt bad about letting him go, but I couldn't see what else I could have done under the circumstances." Although their parting was angry, Miles did tell John he could return to the band if he cleaned up his act.

For a short time after leaving Miles, John did not work much. He continued to smoke cigarettes, drink alcohol, and use heroin.

Finally, he came to a stark realization: Drugs and alcohol were ruining his health, his personal life, and his music. John made a decision to change. He would draw on the strength he had garnered from his readings in religion and philosophy, cleanse himself, and dedicate his music to God.

He told Naima of his decision: "I've decided to stop smoking, drinking and taking drugs. But I need your help. I can't do this all by myself." There was a long pause. "Will you help me, Naima? Will you back me up all the way?"

Naima was overjoyed. "You *know* I will," she said.

John went into his mother's room and had the same conversation with her. His mother was ecstatic, but also anxious to make sure her son followed through on this promise. She said, "John, let's do it now, let's not wait another minute."

John agreed. He went first to the bathroom to clean up, then he went to his room, declaring that he would live on water alone until his system was clear of drugs and alcohol. He would not come out of his room until he had recovered.

For days, John left his room only to go to the bathroom. Naima and Alice worried and prayed. From time to time, they knocked on his door to ask if he was all right. He would either say "yes" or ask for some water.

John was a private person, not one to complain or feel sorry for himself. But Naima and Alice knew that he was suffering in that room, sweating out his withdrawal with none of the crutches he had depended on before.

He would later say that his religious faith helped him through this difficult time. "During the year 1957, I experienced, by the grace of God, a spiritual awakening which was to lead me to a richer, fuller, more productive life," he said. "At that time, in gratitude, I humbly asked to be given the means and privilege to make others happy through music."

Naima also tried to help John lose weight, although he never totally kicked his habit of overeating. He also never quit smoking for good, because he found that when he did not smoke, he ate more. Instead of cigarettes, he eventually turned to cigars, then to pipes. But he was at least able to stay off of drugs and alcohol.

To keep himself from turning back to drugs and alcohol, John practiced his saxophone more than ever. He usually practiced alone, because most of his musician friends were still using heroin, and he did not want to be tempted again.

His hard work and persistence paid off. He was given another chance—this time to play with another of the geniuses of modern jazz, Thelonious Monk.

Monk was a trailblazer and pioneer of the new music, a piano player who sometimes banged on his keyboard as if they were drums. He incorporated sudden starts and stops, unexpected silences and jagged rhythms into his playing and composition. Some thought his music sounded weird and sinister. Like John, he, too, was born in North Carolina, but grew up in New York's Harlem neighborhood.

John had played with Monk on several occasions and even recorded one song with him while he was still with Miles Davis. In fact, Monk had been backstage when Miles had punched John.

John joined the Thelonious Monk Quartet, which, in addition to John on sax and Monk on piano, featured a bass player and a drummer. The quartet had an extended gig at the Five Spot, a club in Manhattan's East Village. Six nights a week, John put on a suit and tie and took the subway to the Five Spot, where the band played to about 150 people packed into the small, smoky room.

Thelonious Monk, a famous jazz pianist, invited John to play saxophone in his band, the Thelonious Monk Quartet. *(Library of Congress)*

Monk had a wispy beard and often wore a fur hat when he played. His music drew the audience to their feet, dancing in the aisles. Often Monk would get up from the piano, whirl and pivot and stomp his feet in time to the beat, and, waving his hands, jump right into the crowd and shuffle dance along with them, leaving John and the rest of the band onstage playing. Sometimes Monk even wandered into the kitchen and struck up conversations with the kitchen help. John found these habits disturbing at first, but he adjusted to leading the band when Monk was not onstage. This helped him grow as a musician and a band leader.

The crowd who came to see Monk was diverse: black and white, young and old, famous and ordinary. David Amram, who had been impressed with John when he played with Miles, showed up to hear him with Monk's group. He was surprised at the progress John had made. "Trane was getting into different harmonic textures, pouring out such a cascade of notes that he was attracting the audience's attention as much as Monk," Amram said. "A lot of musicians were there, digging Monk at first, then commenting more and more on Trane each time they'd come in."

Another famous person who heard the concerts was Willem de Kooning, an abstract expressionist painter. He told Amram that "Coltrane is so different; he's almost like an Einstein of music." Given the fact that John greatly admired Albert Einstein, this was a tremendous compliment.

Naima often came by the Five Spot with a tape recorder. After the concerts, John and Naima sat up into the wee hours of the morning, listening to every detail of John's playing, sometimes rewinding and playing certain sections of the tape over and over again. Often Naima would drift off to sleep while John continued analyzing the tape, always thinking of how his music could be improved.

He was beginning to win over the audiences and the critics, who particularly admired him for holding his own on the stage during Monk's antics. He was highly sought after for recordings, as a leader and as a studio musician for other artists. He even recorded with Sonny Rollins, the man he had replaced in the Miles Davis Quintet. The two men had great respect for each other and even became close friends.

Besides making extra money as a side musician, John also used these opportunities to begin unveiling some songs he had written himself. One was "John Paul Jones," an intricate blues number. He later recorded it again with Miles Davis under the title "Trane's Blues."

Prestige Records offered John a contract for a series of recordings under his own name. The first of these albums, simply titled *Coltrane*, was released on May 31, 1957, with the words "The New Tenor Saxophone Star" printed on the cover. Another record label, Blue Note, also persuaded him to get a temporary release from the Prestige contract to make one album. That album, *Blue Train*, was also well-received.

John was continuing to develop his style and techniques, and he soaked up all he could learn from Monk.

One innovative technique he learned was *multiphonics*, or playing more than one note at once. This was accomplished by using a combination of fingerings and loosening his mouth on the reed.

One of the keys to developing a unique and personal sound on the saxophone is finding the right combination of mouthpiece and the reed. John was always experimenting. Unlike Charlie Parker, who had a reputation of being able to achieve the same sound even on borrowed mouthpieces and instruments, John was very particular about his tools and was not easily satisfied. In his mind he heard certain sounds that he wanted to express, and he collected many different mouthpieces in his attempt to achieve them. Even when he found one he liked, he sometimes had it sanded and adjusted.

Tom Dowd, a recording engineer, witnessed John's quest for perfection.

> John usually showed up about an hour before the [recording] session. Much in the manner of classical musicians practicing before a recital, he would stand in a corner, face the wall, play, stop, change reeds, and start again. After a while he would settle on a mouthpiece and reed that felt most comfortable to him, and then he would start to work on the 'runs' he wanted to use during the session. I would watch him play the same passage over and over again, changing his breathing, his fingering, and experimenting with the most minute changes in his phrasing. Once in a while he

would go back to a mouthpiece he had abandoned earlier.

John's hard work was beginning to pay off. One writer wrote glowing comments in *Jazz Review*:

> What sets Coltrane apart from other tenor players is the equality of strength in all registers which he has obtained through long, hard practice. His sound is just as clear, full and unforced in the topmost notes as it is down at the bottom. Those who say he doesn't play in tune are wrong, deceived by the sharp edge of his sound. He plays in tune—always. That powerful sound of his you hear consists of very long phrases played at such an extremely rapid tempo that the notes he plays cease to be mere notes and fuse into a continuous flow of pure sound.

John's comeback did not go unnoticed by Miles Davis, who now invited him back to his band. But it was a different John Coltrane who rejoined Miles. No longer taking drugs, the new Coltrane was a confident powerhouse of a musician playing with a new vision.

Chapter Five

Giant Steps, Kind of Blue

A new source of tension developed between Miles and John. John now had a solid reputation of his own, as well as a recording contract. He could form his own group and get work in clubs. Playing with Miles meant that he had to put aside his own original material, which he was writing more and more of, to play what Miles wanted. It soon became evident that John would eventually strike out on his own.

Despite the lack of personal closeness between the two men, Miles appreciated John's talent fully and went out of his way to support him, even helping him record some solo albums while he was still with the band. But John felt antsy. He saw other good tenors leaving groups and starting their own bands, and he wanted to do the same.

By now jazz writer Ira Gitler had invented a new phrase to describe John's unique style. He called it "sheets of sound," referring to the way John played several chords at once. The notes pouring out of John's saxophone were "so thick and complex they were almost flowing out of the horn by themselves," Gitler said. "That really hit me, the continuous flow of ideas without stopping. It was almost superhuman, and the amount of energy he was using could have powered a space ship."

John was not content with a few successful albums and good music reviews. He continued practicing constantly and looking for new inspirations. He would often begin a practice session with exercises from a saxophone book, then move on to the *Thesaurus of Scales and Melodic Patterns*, which was used mainly by pianists. From this he would practice endless scales and chord progressions. Then he switched to a violin book in order to absorb classical music influence. Finally, he would end with exercises from a harp book. Because harp music is written for the very highest notes of the treble clef, John could use these exercises to practice hitting the highest possible notes on the tenor saxophone.

He did all of this work alone, using a tape recorder to play back his practice session to critique himself. Many people who knew John thought his constant practicing was extreme. One admirer said, "Whatever he did he did all the way, with no middle ground."

While many appreciated John's innovative style, some critics continued to doubt his talents. They wrote articles using adjectives such as "angry" and "neurotic" to describe his music. One writer even said John's music resembled a barking dog and "epileptic fits of passion." John was particularly bothered by the fact that some people considered his music angry. He told Gitler, "If it is interpreted as angry, it is taken wrong. The only one I'm angry at is myself when I don't make what I'm trying to play." He explained that the reason he played so many sounds at once—something that some listeners interpreted as angry—was because he had so many ideas and so many things he wanted to try, all at the same time.

The conflicting opinions about John's music were evident at live performances. At one concert in Paris, a large part of the audience cheered and clapped and gave him a standing ovation. Another group, however, was booing at the same time.

His second stint with Miles was invaluable. The group, enlarged to a sextet with the addition of alto saxophonist Cannonball Adderly, is still today the most famous and influential small group in jazz history. In the years 1959 and 1960, John would participate in the recording of two of the most famous jazz albums ever recorded: *Kind of Blue*, recorded with Miles, and *Giant Steps*, which John recorded for Atlantic, his new label, with his own band.

Kind of Blue is one of the most influential albums of the twentieth century. Thousands of copies are still sold every year. The musicians who gathered to record the songs in a studio in two sessions in March and April of 1959, including Miles and John, knew that they were trying a new method to play improvised music. But they had no way of knowing that the music they produced would be so groundbreaking.

The musicians did not play from sheet music or improvise on the chords of favorite songs, which was the principal way most bop jazz was performed. Instead, each musician developed melodies from a set of scales Miles sketched out only a few hours before he went into the studio. The scales provided only a general framework for them to improvise from. Bill Evans, the pianist at the session, gave an explanation of the framework of each song in the album's liner notes: "*So What* is a simple figure based on 16 measures of one scale, 8 of another and 8 more of the first, following a piano and bass introduction in free rhythm style . . . *Flamenco Sketches* is a series of five scales, each to be played as long as the soloist wishes until he has completed the series."

Of course, since they did not exist on paper, none of the musicians had ever played any of the pieces before. With a group of lesser talent, this would have been disastrous—or at least an album that required many, many retakes. Miraculously, for most of the five pieces on the album, the first complete performance of each ended up being the take used for the album. Of all the players in the group, none made more of an impression with his solos than the tenor saxophonist. Even for those who had not previously liked Coltrane's music, it was difficult to deny that his breathtaking solos on *Kind of Blue* were works of passionate, wild beauty.

The most significant innovation on *Kind of Blue* was the use of *modes*, or series of scales, instead of the usual sequence of chords or harmonies to perform.

Although Miles did not invent this technique, *Kind of Blue* marked the first time that the majority of jazz listeners had ever heard an entire album that used modes. Although modal jazz sounds like a complicated concept, it was actually an approach that *simplified* jazz by returning to emphasizing a song's basic *melody* instead of chords.

Miles had complained about chords in a 1958 interview: "The music has gotten thick. Guys give me tunes and they're full of chords. I can't play them. I think a movement in jazz is beginning away from the conventional string of chords, and a return to emphasis on melodic rather than harmonic variation. There will be fewer chords but infinite possibilities as to what to do with them."

Kind of Blue remains one of the warmest and most romantic jazz albums ever recorded. Many people who own only a few jazz albums claim *Kind of Blue* as one of them. The modal jazz technique was a concept that deeply influenced John Coltrane. He would actively explore it and test its limits in his own music for the rest of his life.

In the meantime, though, John continued playing "thick" music on his own albums. Instead of removing chords he found ways to play even more chords as he continued to experiment with "sheets of sound" in his first landmark album, *Giant Steps*. One technique that fascinated him was emphasizing third-related chord movements. "Thirds" is a term that refers to the interval spanning three consecutive notes in a scale, such as C-

E or D-F. It also describes the note three scale steps higher than the root of the chord. In the chord C-E-G, E is the third. The concept of thirds is not unique to jazz; the great classical composer Ludwig von Beethoven used this technique in his work.

John explored this concept fully in the album's title track, a song "that knocked the jazz world on its ear," according to one writer. John wrote all seven outstanding compositions on the album, and his playing on them all was phenomenal. Another song was "Naima," a serene slow ballad John wrote as a tribute to his wife. It would remain his favorite composition, and a crowd favorite, for the rest of his life.

There were two other tributes on the album to important women in his life. "Syeeda's Song Flute" was a bouncy tune honoring his stepdaughter and her recorder, an inexpensive plastic instrument sometimes also referred to as a "song flute." Another piece, "Cousin Mary," was a blues song honoring his beloved cousin. There was also "Mr. P.C.," a dedication to bass player Paul Chambers, and "Like Sonny," a tribute to saxophonist Sonny Rollins that showed influences from Latin and African rhythms.

John encouraged young musicians who were struggling to succeed. If he saw some of them sitting at a table at one of his club dates, he would stop by to talk with them during intermission. On another occasion, his two young nephews were performing at a jazz club in South Philadelphia when they realized, much to their surprise, that Uncle John Coltrane was sitting quietly in the audience. At intermission, John's nephews were proud when John walked up to the stage and talked with them, right in front of everyone.

This spirit of kindness was typical of John Coltrane. Despite his growing fame, he remained humble and sincere. In some ways, his unassuming nature hindered his popularity, because other more outgoing and publicity-seeking artists received more press coverage and exposure than he did.

Another thing that had not changed was John's love of food—particularly sweet potato pie, pizza and Butter Rum Life Savers—and the continuing problems with his weight and his teeth. He finally forced himself to go to the dentist again, where he heard the grim news that his teeth were so rotten that many would have to be pulled and replaced with bridgework.

He continued to alternate between overeating and dieting, and his weight sometimes seesawed by thirty pounds. Finally Naima and his friends persuaded him to eat more health foods, such as nutrition bars, raw vegetables, organically grown fruit, and all kinds of beans. He began eating more often at Indian restaurants, too, which seemed to fit with his growing interest in Indian music and the writings of Eastern philosophers. Somehow in the midst of all of his performing and practicing, he found time to read these books, as well as others about space travel and Albert Einstein. When visitors came to his home, they sometimes played music, but other times they discussed gravity, electromagnetic attraction, and Einstein's Theory of Relativity.

John also had a new musical interest: the soprano saxophone, a small, straight horn that resembled a clarinet. For years John had been pushing the tenor saxophone to its upper limit, and now the soprano allowed him to achieve even higher sounds.

John's impulsive eating, practicing, and musical experimenting sometimes frustrated Naima. "I had to separate the musician from the man in order for me to live with him," she once said. One day John brought a harp home and set it in the corner of the living room. Half-jokingly and half-seriously, he began nagging Naima to learn how to play it—something she had no interest in doing.

Finally, in 1960, John took the ultimate step out on his own. He formed his own band, the John Coltrane Quartet.

In addition to John on tenor sax, the other members played piano, bass, and drums. The group gave him a platform to explore his own musical ideas, but it also brought on more responsibility. Now it was John who had to hire and fire band members. He made a few mistakes, hiring musicians whom he then had to fire because they were not playing the way he wanted. It took several months and a few false starts before he arrived at the ideal combination: Elvin Jones on drums, Steve Davis on bass, and McCoy Tyner on piano. In addition to playing well together, the men also became close friends.

John had to wait for Elvin Jones to finish serving a jail term before he could play. He hired him only after

Elvin assured him he had stopped using drugs. It took only a few minutes of listening to Elvin's drumming to understand why John wanted him in the band so badly.

Steve Davis described Elvin's playing:

> That first night Elvin was in the band, he was playing so strong and so loud you could hear him outside the club and down the block. But Trane wanted it that way. He wanted a drummer who could really kick, and Elvin was one of the strongest, wildest drummers in the world. After the gig, Trane put his arm around Elvin, took him to a barbecue place around the corner, and bought him some ribs. Trane and Elvin were tight from then on.

Unlike the other three musicians, who showed little emotion while performing, Elvin grinned and grunted as he attacked the drums.

The band traveled the country in John's Mercury station wagon to play clubs in large cities such as Detroit and Chicago. John usually drove, but one night as the band left Denver he decided to let Elvin take over while he napped in the back seat. Steve and McCoy were sleeping, too, until Steve, who was in the front passenger seat, awoke and was alarmed by Elvin's driving.

"I looked at the speedometer and Elvin was doing 90, he was working out on the steering wheel and accelerator like a set of drums," Steve said. "I woke up

McCoy and he woke up John, and the two of us talked John into taking over the wheel again."

On another occasion, Elvin borrowed the car to go on a date. After dropping the woman off, Elvin drove too fast and skidded off the road, hitting a tree. Fortunately, John was understanding about the accident. "The car was a total wreck, but I walked away with just bruises and scratches," Elvin later recalled. "When I told Trane about it he said, 'I can always get another car, but there's only one Elvin.' "

During only one week in October 1960, the quartet recorded so much material that it eventually formed not one, but three, albums: *My Favorite Things*, which was released in March 1961; *Coltrane Plays the Blues*, is-

Coltrane chose Elvin Jones, a passionate and dynamic drummer, to play in his jazz band. *(Library of Congress)*

sued in 1962; and *Coltrane's Sound*, not released until 1964.

The title song from *My Favorite Things* featured John playing soprano sax. The soprano sax had once been a popular jazz instrument—Sidney Bechet, an early jazz musician from New Orleans—had recorded on it in the 1920s and 1930s, but it had been out of favor for years until Coltrane began playing it again. "My Favorite Things" is best known for being sung by actress Julie Andrews in the movie *The Sound of Music*, but John's jazz version made a strong impression.

The album *My Favorite Things* sold 50,000 copies within a year after its release. The average jazz album sold only 5,000 copies. The *San Francisco Examiner* proclaimed it Coltrane's best at the time and ultimately one of the most important albums of the 1960s.

In an interview with *Down Beat*, an influential magazine read by jazz musicians and fans, John explained his philosophy and the fact that he was continuously studying, striving to find new ways of expressing himself: "I've found you've got to look back at the old things and see them in a new light. I'm not finished with these studies because I haven't assimilated everything into my playing." He also spoke of his struggle to please himself while satisfying the fans and music critics. "I want to progress, but I don't want to go so far out that I can't see what others are doing."

His fan base grew rapidly, and many other jazz musicians were beginning to imitate his style. *Down Beat* named him "Jazzman of the Year" in 1961. The magazine's readers, as well as the international critics, named him best tenor saxophonist and best miscellaneous instrumentalist (for soprano sax). Readers and critics also gave him high marks in England's *Melody Maker* magazine.

But John took his new fame in stride. He did not place that much importance on the ratings. "But, on the other hand, it makes me aware of being surrounded by a certain number of people who have confidence in me, and that I must not disappoint them, in any way, in order to show my gratitude," he said.

Still, pleasing crowds was not John's primary motive. His first goal was to play the music the way he wanted to express it. "If this [success] happened to me without [achieving] what I personally wanted, I wouldn't sacrifice my personal search for the satisfaction of my fans," he said.

"There are still many things I want to do; all that remains for me to desire is to continue to find people who like my music in the course of its evolution," he continued. "I believe that it would not be honest for me to stop because I've found a big enough audience to get me a good place in the polls. However, I was very happy to see that I am able to touch an extended public, because I have always had to resolve the problem of communication with my listeners."

John saw his music as a way to make a statement, to be a force for good, to make other people's lives more meaningful through music. It was a quest he would pursue earnestly for the rest of his life.

Chapter Six

Chasin' the Trane

John continued to battle his weight problems, alternating between strict dieting and binges of delicacies such as sweet potato pie. This had become such a routine that he now owned two entirely separate wardrobes: one for when he was thin, the other for when he was overweight.

Musically, his career continued to flourish, although his unique style continued to confuse some listeners and critics. Overall, however, his fans far outnumbered his detractors.

One triumph was John's first European tour with his own band, particularly his return to the Olympia Theater in Paris. A year before, when he had played there with Miles, a significant minority of the crowd had booed and hissed at John's saxophone solos. By contrast, during this tour, John was mobbed for autographs when he went to eat dinner between shows.

The rest of the tour covered England, Germany, and Scandinavia. In Europe, more people seemed to understand that John's music was serious art. The band members played their hearts out, inspired by the crowds, who clapped and stomped their feet to show their appreciation.

There were a few boos and negative reviews during this concert tour. In England, the reviews were especially bad. Much of the criticism this time centered around Eric Dolphy, a musician John had added to the group just before the tour began. Dolphy was an excellent musician who could play alto saxophone, flute, and bass clarinet—and play all of them well. He had his own style that many people did not understand. He was a free spirit who liked to play his flute to emulate the sounds of birds. Sometimes he did not bother to create a melody or to stick to any recognizable tune. Other times, he repeated the same passage of music over and over again, slightly varying the pitch of a single note. This aggravated some critics, who accused him of arrogance for disregarding his audience.

Nonetheless, John stood by Eric, just as Miles Davis had done for him. Eric did finally leave the group, but not because John asked him to. John remained his friend and kept him working as a studio sideman until Dolphy's death a few years later.

In 1961, John signed a contract with yet another major label, Impulse Records, which had been created by American Broadcasting Company. John's popularity justified an advance fee of $50,000, a phenomenal amount for a jazz band. It was the first time that John had complete control of not only the music, but also the packaging, graphics, and layout of the album covers.

Impulse included extra space in record albums for photos and liner notes. For this, the company charged $5.98 an album, a dollar more than most jazz records, but this did not stop the public from buying them. John's first album for Impulse Records was called *Africa/Brass* and included African rhythms and Indian ragas. This was the beginning of a very successful partnership between John and producer Bob Thiele. Thiele, a stocky, pipe-smoking man, was interested in John and other musicians who were playing what he called the "New Black Music," music with artistic freedom expressed through flexible rhythms and intense improvising.

Sometimes John recorded his live performances. One night, he prepared to record a blues song that illustrated a true example of how well he and his group had achieved the art of improvising. The unnamed song was not written down. The band just started with a short tune based on a composition by the classical composer Debussy, set a tempo, and away they went.

What followed next was fifteen minutes and fifty-five seconds of the musicians improvising a stream-of-consciousness tune that left some people just shaking their heads and others astounded. Bob Thiele was tapping his feet and puffing so hard on his pipe that he surrounded himself in a shroud of smoke. The sound engineer literally ran around the club after John, trying his best to keep the microphone positioned near John's saxophone, even if it meant climbing over people in the audience. When it was finally over, no one could figure

Eric Dolphy played a number of instruments in Coltrane's band.
(Library of Congress)

out what to call the song, but the sound engineer thought of a very fitting title to describe what he had been doing all night: "Chasin' the Trane."

The recording was another milestone in John's career, though not without alienating some fans and critics. Ira Gitler, the jazz writer who had so strongly supported Coltrane's efforts, wrote: "Coltrane may be searching for a new avenue of expression, but if it is going to take this form of yawps, squawks, and countless repetitive runs, then it should be confined to the woodshed."

John was also a leader in the new "world music" movement. He continued exposing himself to the music of other cultures—particularly India, Africa, and Latin America—and incorporating those influences in his own compositions. By this time he was recording as often as possible. His contract called for only two albums a year, but he amassed so much material in 1962 alone that Impulse Records put out three that year. Much of it was recorded in the studio in the wee hours of the morning.

The album *Coltrane* was the first to be released. It featured a song, "Out of This World," in which John played a long solo deliberately out of tempo from the rest of the band.

Thiele began to worry that many of John's recent controversial recordings would alienate his mainstream fans. At Thiele's urging, John recorded two more traditional albums, *Ballads* and *John Coltrane & Johnny Hartman*, the second featuring a popular singer. John

Coltrane paired up with jazz legend Duke Ellington to record an album.
(Library of Congress)

was easily persuaded to do these albums, because he continued to love traditional ballads even while he pushed the envelope with his other music. It also gave him a chance to use a mouthpiece that he said he had ruined, through all his tinkering, for playing fast music.

Thiele had another brilliant idea for an album as well: pairing John with the great Duke Ellington. Thiele hoped that, by playing together, the two would stimulate each other's creativity. He was right. *Duke Ellington and John Coltrane* turned out to be a success, and Ellington had a positive influence on John as well, helping him accept the fact that he did not have to always record several takes of the same song.

After they had recorded only one take of "In a Sentimental Mood," Thiele asked, "Duke, what do you think?"

The Duke replied, "That's fine."

Then Thiele asked, "John, do you think we should do it again or not?"

John hesitated. "Well . . ."

The Duke interrupted. "Why play it again? You can't duplicate that feeling. This is it."

When many others heard it later, they agreed. One of them was John's idol Johnny Hodges, who had played the song many times when he was part of the Duke's band. "I think Coltrane gave the most beautiful interpretation I've ever heard," he said.

John continued playing clubs as well. One of them was Birdland, named for Charlie Parker and located in the basement of a building at Broadway and 53rd Street in New York City. It was at that club that John came to know an up-and-coming young comedian named Bill Cosby.

Cosby was fascinated by the way John put such passion and energy into his saxophone playing, and he secretly began practicing an imitation of him. While Cosby did not play the saxophone, he posed as if he had one in his hand, holding his mouth as though it contained a mouthpiece, and moving his fingers over imaginary saxophone keys, then humming strange sounds from his throat to imitate John's playing.

John, who was humble enough to laugh at himself, let Cosby do this imitation to entertain the audience while he took breaks from playing. The imitation be-

Comedian Bill Cosby became well-known for imitating Coltrane during his jazz shows. *(Library of Congress)*

came more and more elaborate. One night Cosby stood on the stage, pretending to play the saxophone and wailing the tune "Out of This World" exactly the way Coltrane had recorded it. Then Cosby bent down in a crouch, and his face took on an exuberant, sweating look just like John's. On and on he went, humming and screeching the song, alone on the stage for four minutes. The audience roared with laughter.

All of a sudden, from backstage, came John, playing his saxophone note for note to match Bill Cosby. Cosby looked stunned at first, but he continued on, as John came and stood just a few inches away, playing his sax. The audience roared and clapped at this strange "duet."

John faced difficulties in his personal life. The long hours of practicing and years of traveling had taken their toll on his marriage. Naima felt disconnected from her husband. Conversation did not come as easily; they did not communicate the way they had before.

In an attempt to make things normal again, she went along with John and the band on their European tour in November 1962. Although it was Naima's first trip to Europe, John did not take time out of his busy schedule to show her the sights. He was busy writing, rehearsing, playing, and being interviewed.

Then, in the summer of 1963, John moved out of the house he had shared with Naima and Syeeda. Although she was upset, Naima was not surprised. "He didn't offer any explanation. He just told me there were some things he had to do, and he left with only his clothes and his horns. He stayed in a hotel sometimes, other times with his mother in Philadelphia. All he said was, 'Naima, I'm going to make a change.' Even though I could feel it coming, it hurt, and I didn't get over it for at least another year."

John would always have a soft spot in his heart for Naima, however, and the song he had written and named for her remained his personal favorite.

That September, a tragedy shocked the nation and affected John deeply. One Sunday morning in Birmingham, Alabama, twelve sticks of dynamite exploded in the basement of a black church. The explosion blew holes in the walls, injured fourteen people, and killed four girls, ages eleven to fourteen, who had just finished their Sunday school lesson.

John was overcome with sadness when he heard the news on the radio. He deeply believed that people should love and respect one another, and although racism was obvious all around him, he could not believe that someone would go so far as to kill innocent churchgoers in the name of hatred.

He put his grief to music and recorded a eulogy, "Alabama," about the tragedy, which was released on his *Birdland* album. His sadness was shared by millions of people throughout the country, many of them increasingly angry about the long years of segregation and racism. The Alabama church bombing would become a seminal event in the Civil Rights Movement.

But John's sadness was not confined only to problems such as these. Although he had always been a quiet man, his friends were now noticing that he also appeared sad and melancholy at times, and this was evident in his music as well.

He was also becoming more attuned to helping young musicians get started. During his gigs at the Half Note, a New York City jazz club that was well known for its casual atmosphere, he would frequently let young musicians come up on the stage and play a few numbers. Sometimes members of the audience who had come to see John complained about having to listen to mere amateurs. But John had a ready answer from the bandstand: "Well, these young musicians have to start someplace, like I did. You don't think I just walked up to Miles or Monk and got the job like that, do you?"

His spirituality came through to those who heard him play, both on recordings and in person. J. C. Thomas, a friend of Coltrane's who later wrote a biography of him, described Coltrane's spirituality:

> John Coltrane was more mystic than musician. This is the only logical explanation for the effects his music had on many members of his audience; in fact, many of them knew nothing whatsoever about any kind of music, including jazz, yet they were mesmerized, entranced. There had to be something else besides music there; in reality, there was a force beyond music that was communicating with Trane's audience on quite a different, higher level of being. Call it Universal Consciousness, Supreme Being, Nature, God. Call this force by any name you like, but it was *there*.

Chapter Seven

It Ended All Too Soon

Throughout his career John had many fans, but there was always a significant group who criticized his music. He became even more controversial as the 1960s developed. He left bop jazz behind and continued to experiment with harmonic freedom and avant-garde techniques. He was interested in writing music that was "atonal," without a tone at all, or experimenting with choosing a certain note—for example C—as the tonal center and playing freely around it.

Many people were bothered by the fact that John's pieces had evolved to the point that they were no longer "tunes" in the traditional sense; they often did not have memorable melodies that could be easily hummed. The fans who stuck by him were those who appreciated his concentrated and focused discipline, his intricate improvising and new ideas, and the energy and passion he poured out of his music.

In concert, John's solos were getting longer and longer. It was not unusual for one to last an hour—one was even said to have lasted *three* hours. John was overflowing with ideas he wanted to express, and he wanted to develop them fully to their logical end. He told a French magazine, "When some evenings, in beginning to play, we feel inspired and we foresee the possibility of realizing good things, it seems illogical and unreasonable for us to shorten our solos. My ideas have to develop themselves naturally in a long solo."

Many people who had not appreciated his music before, however, were intrigued by an album he released in 1964 called *A Love Supreme*. It touched many listeners on a deeply spiritual level. *A Love Supreme* remains John's most popular solo album, selling half a million copies by 1970 and many more since then. In addition to recording the music, John also wrote a poem by the same name that was printed in the liner notes.

A Love Supreme contained four sections— "Acknowledgement," "Resolution," "Pursuance," and "Psalm." Each section attempted to reveal the stages of a spiritual journey in which a man acknowledges a divine presence, resolves to pursue it, then eventually celebrates its presence. John made the recording at a difficult time in his life, a time of searching. It had been only a few months since he had left Naima, and the guilt from ending his marriage still lingered. In fact, he wrote about this in the liner notes of the album: "I entered into a phase which was contradictory to the pledge [to God] and away from the esteemed path."

It seemed that John was thinking about his own mortality as well. One friend, Robin Kenyatta, recalled having an odd conversation with him outside the Birdland Club right after he had recorded *A Love Supreme*.

> He was talking about death in a philosophical
> way, just like it was a subject of ordinary
> conversation. I was young, in my twenties,
> and he scared me. I said, 'Why talk about
> death, when there's so many beautiful things
> in life?' I tried to move the conversation back
> to music, but he would keep bringing up the
> subject of death every few minutes. I think he
> must have known then that something was
> wrong and that he wouldn't have long to live.

Another friend, Bobby Timmons, had a disturbing
conversation with John's mother, who said her son had
seen a vision of God just before he composed *A Love
Supreme*. She was worried about this and even said that
she wished John had never written the album. "When
someone is seeing God, that means he's going to die,"
she told Timmons.

At the same time, John was falling in love again, this
time with a piano player, Alice McLeod. Perhaps John
felt that she truly understood his music and the overwhelming presence it had in his life.

Alice regarded their relationship in a philosophical
and spiritual way. "We were both traveling in a particular spiritual direction, John and myself, so it seemed
only natural for us to join forces," she said later. "It was
like God uniting two souls together. I think John could
have just as easily married another woman, though. Not
myself and not because I was a musician, but any woman
who had the particular attributes or qualities to help

him fulfill his life mission as God wanted him to."

Alice had been born in Detroit, the fifth of six children. She learned to play the piano at a young age and played it for her church, where she also sang in the choir. As a young woman, she studied classical piano in Manhattan and Paris. By 1962, she was becoming a real fixture in Detroit clubs, playing bebop on piano and a small portable organ called an "organa." Alice could also play the vibraphone, a percussion instrument with tuned metal bars that were played with a soft padded hammer.

Alice and John married in Mexico in August 1966. Like her husband, Alice was quiet, shy, and very serious about music. Their relationship produced three children: John W. Coltrane Jr., Ravi John Coltrane (named for Indian sitar player Ravi Shankar), and Oranyan Olabisi Coltrane, known as Oran. Alice began playing piano with John's group and also learned to play the harp, something that made John happy.

John continued his intense study of music from around the world. He listened to recordings of bells of worship in Buddhist temples, Japanese worship music, and music from Africa and Brazil. Alice described his deep interest in music from other cultures:

> He researched, he investigated all the musics
> of the world, because he knew that everyone
> had something. Sometimes he would travel.
> And he would bring back, I mean, a whole
> case of books, tapes, records. That is what he

John's experimental music brought him both praise and criticism. *(© Burt and Katherine Holzman Goldblatt)*

did, and sometimes he would have to ship things home. Ravi Shankar did invite him to come to India. Of course that never came to being, but I'm sure that would have been quite an interesting spiritual and musical experience.

As it turned out, John's new quintet, including Alice on piano, was his most controversial yet. The band played with almost no steady beat, totally freeform. Even Ravi Shankar, who came to see the group play, was supportive but puzzled. He said:

I was much disturbed by his music. Here was a creative person who had become a vegetarian,

> who was studying yoga and reading the
> Bhagavad-Gita [a 700-verse sacred poem of
> the Hindu faith], yet in whose music I still
> heard much turmoil. I could not understand it.
> There was a turbulence in the music that gave
> me a negative feeling at times, but I could not
> quite put my finger on the trouble.

Others were even more critical. When the band arrived at Temple University in 1966 to play a concert, they were greeted warmly by an overflowing crowd of mostly students, both black and white. But the band's first tune lasted an hour, too long for many of the fans who had stuck with Coltrane through the years. As the show progressed, more and more people walked out.

One of those who remained was Frances Davis, who recalled that night in a *Village Voice* article in 1992. Not only did the crowd represent the division over John Coltrane's music, but over the direction of jazz in general, she said.

"Those who walked out on him in Philadelphia did so thinking that he had, in effect, already walked out on them by turning his band into an open forum for a despised and divisive avant-garde," Davis wrote. "Coltrane had been the magic figure of consensus—the man in whose music recent tradition and the urge to explore further reached a workable truce. I was one of the people up on my feet and cheering at the end of that Temple concert, and I still am. But I think I realized even then that if those of us devoted to jazz could no longer agree on Coltrane, we were never going to agree on anything else again."

John was troubled by this, but he also knew he could not turn back. "When he became avant-garde, as they termed it, he lost many people, many followers," Alice said. "They didn't like it, they didn't approve of it, they didn't appreciate it. And there was no way he could go back, there was no road to return on. It was his commitment, it was his decision."

John himself said, "Whenever I make a change, I'm a little worried that it might puzzle people. And sometimes I deliberately delay things for this reason. But after a while I find that there is nothing else I can do but go ahead."

Some of John's most devoted fans were not even in the United States. When the band's airplane landed for its tour of Japan, it was greeted by a mob of fans cheering and holding life-size posters and cut-outs of John and the other musicians. They walked from the plane into the airport terminal on red carpet that had been rolled out in their honor.

After the band's first concert in Tokyo, John was mobbed for autographs. When he thought he was finally finished and climbed into a taxicab, a young boy came running up just as the cab pulled away. As the cab rolled down the street, Alice looked back to see the young boy, still running. A little while later, there was a knock on the door of the Coltranes' hotel room. It was the same boy, who had apparently run many blocks to get an autograph.

During the Japan tour, John took the time to visit the War Memorial Park in Nagasaki, where the second atomic bomb of World War II had killed more than 150,000 Japanese people in 1945. He bowed his head, prayed for the dead, and asked God for world peace.

The year before, *Down Beat* magazine had once again proclaimed John "Jazzman of the Year," elected him to the Hall of Fame, gave him first place on tenor saxophone, and named *A Love Supreme* as "Record of the Year." But there was an interesting difference of opinion among the critics. While sixty-four percent of the European judges voted for John as best tenor, only one third of the American and Canadian critics gave him that honor. A year later, *Swing Journal*, a Japanese magazine devoted to jazz, voted him the most popular musician in Japan.

From her piano onstage, Alice observed some fans responding to John's music in a very spiritual and worshipful way. "Someone in the audience would stand up, their arms upreaching, and they would be like that for an hour or more," she said. "Their clothing would be soaked with perspiration, and when they finally sat down, they practically fell down. The music just took people out of the whole material world; it lifted them up."

But John was slipping away. When he returned from the very successful Japan tour, the agent George Wein called and asked him to tour Europe again in the fall. "He said he wasn't feeling well, and he really sounded tired, so I offered to pace the tour any way he wanted,"

Wein said later. "He said he wasn't sure he wanted to go, that he was feeling weak. When I asked him why, he said, 'I'm not eating.' I was shocked; I asked him what kind of diet he was on. He said, 'I'm not on any diet; I'm just not eating.'" John then explained to George that he was trying to "clean out his system."

John was also taking handfuls of aspirin for the bad headaches he was having. This alarmed Alice, who insisted he go to the doctor. John waved her off, saying he would be all right.

He told one of his friends, Babatunde Olatunji, or "Tunji" for short, that he was growing weary of constant touring. "I'm used to the critics complaining about me, and sooner or later they should understand my music," John told Tunji. "If they don't, there's nothing I can do about it. But what's really bothering me is the way I have to move around, New York today, Detroit tomorrow, San Francisco the day after that. It seems to me that I've been using up so much energy traveling from place to place that I hardly can find time for writing any new music or even thinking about what I'm going to do next."

Tunji told John of his dream of building an African cultural center in New York City. The center would include a room where John and other musicians, even amateurs, could rehearse and perform without paying any rental fees. John invested some of his own money and also agreed to give benefit concerts to raise money for the center.

Such a large crowd turned out to see the first concert

in April 1967 that John played one set to a full house, then emptied the room so that another group could come in.

Rashied Ali, who was playing drums for the band at that time, noticed that although John's saxophone playing was as strong as ever, he now spent more time sitting down while playing. John also had added another tenor saxophonist to play alongside him in the band. John explained: "It helps me stay alive sometimes, because physically, man, the pace I've been leading has been so hard and I've gained so much weight, that sometimes it's been a little hard physically. I feel that I like to have somebody there in case I can't get that strength. I like to have that strength in the band, somewhere."

He seriously contemplated taking a total break from performing, perhaps teaching instead. His cousin Mary also noticed something surprising about John: Although his weight remained high, he was still eating very little.

By May of 1967, John was complaining of severe pain around his stomach. He went into the hospital and had a biopsy that revealed liver cancer, perhaps the delayed result of the many years of drug and alcohol abuse. Although his doctor wanted to operate immediately, John rejected this idea. The chances of curing it were slim.

Instead, he went home and spent many days at a time stretched out on the couch, listening to his many recording sessions. There were also a number of recordings he had made in the studio that had not yet been released, and he met with Bob Thiele about those just a few days before he went into the hospital for the last time.

On July 17, 1967, two months before he would have turned forty-one, John passed away in the hospital. His friends and family were shocked and overwhelmed with grief. Miles Davis commented on the suddenness of the death: "Coltrane's death shocked everyone, took everyone by surprise. I knew he hadn't looked too good and had gained a lot of weight the last time I saw him. But I didn't know he was that sick—or even sick at all. I think only a few people really knew that he was sick. Trane kept everything close to his vest."

Alice recalled that, even while John laid on the couch, he said very little about feeling sick. His stunned friends pored over in their minds the last time they had seen him, the last time they had talked with him, trying to remember if there had been any clues that he was dying. One thing that struck them was how passionate and spiritual he and his music had become in his last years.

A week after his death, 1,000 people gathered at St. Peter's Church in Manhattan to pay their last respects. His friend Calvin Massey read the poem "A Love Supreme" that John had written. Jazz musicians Ornette Coleman and Albert Ayler, along with their respective quartets, played one number each.

Coltrane's sons carried on his legacy. John Jr. played the bass until he was killed in a car accident in 1982. Oran studied at the California Institute of the Arts and played the alto saxophone for a long time.

Although he was only a toddler when his father passed away, it was Ravi who has most closely followed in Coltrane's footsteps. He has been critically acclaimed for his skill on the tenor saxophone and has recorded with a number of other artists. "When I discovered jazz, I discovered it on my own," he said. "There was a point when it was the son listening to his father to figure out what his father was about. Later I was a musician listening to John Coltrane to find out what music is about."

John Coltrane influenced many young alto and tenor saxophonists. He was one of the most influential jazz musicians of the last fifty years. Each new saxophonist in jazz has to contend with his legacy. Jazz, however, has never recovered the dominance it had held over the American music scene. The explosive popularity of rock 'n' roll overwhelmed jazz. Most of the jazz clubs in the major cities are no longer open.

But John's impact stretched across the divide to other forms of music. The Beatles, for example, shared his appreciation of Ravi Shankar's sitar playing. "Within You Without You" from the *Sgt. Pepper's Lonely Hearts Club Band* album, as well as "Tomorrow Never Knows" and "Love You To" from the Beatles' *Revolver* album, reflect this influence.

The Byrds, the Allman Brothers, Eric Clapton, and The Who are among many groups who have credited John Coltrane as an influence on their music. Carlos Santana, Bono of the Irish rock group U2, and the late Jerry Garcia of the Grateful Dead have also proclaimed themselves devoted fans. U2's song "Angel of Harlem," released in 1988, mentions John Coltrane and *A Love Supreme*. Other writers and artists have said they listen to his music as they create their own art. The title character in the 1996 movie "Mr. Holland's Opus" names his son after John Coltrane.

In San Francisco, the One Mind Evolutionary Transitional Church of Christ uses music from *A Love Supreme* in its worship services and hosts a weekly radio program of John's recordings. The members of the church worship Jesus but see John Coltrane as an example of someone who experienced redemption during his life.

Naima, John's first wife, passed away in 1996. Alice Coltrane has forsaken performing but still organizes John Coltrane festivals in Los Angeles—two days of concerts held around John's birthday each year.

In High Point, North Carolina, where John grew up, a historical marker describes him as "a world-renowned jazz legend whose warm and lyrical style influences generations of artists." A museum collection there also pays tribute to John Coltrane and was recently visited by his son Ravi. In 1995, the U.S. Postal Service issued a series of ten postage stamps featuring jazz artists, and one was dedicated to John Coltrane.

In Philadelphia, where John blossomed as a young jazz musician, his cousin Mary and six other women formed the John W. Coltrane Cultural Society in the house where she and John once lived. The home has been designated an historic building, and the society sponsors concerts, music workshops, and lectures that continue John Coltrane's legacy. "In this way, I am sharing John's life with the children," Mary said.

Perhaps it is a plaque on a building in Hamlet, where John was born, that best describes his impact:

JOHN COLTRANE
"A Jazz Messiah"
WAS BORN *HERE* 9-23-26
DIED 7-17-67

Discography

1956—*John Coltrane: The Prestige Recordings,*
    Prestige
1957—*Blue Trane*, Blue Note
    Coltrane, Original Jazz
    Round about Midnight with the Miles Davis
    Quintet, Columbia Records
 1959—*Giant Steps*, Atlantic
    Kind of Blue, Atlantic
    *Heavyweight Champion: The Complete Atlantic
    Recordings*, Atlantic
1961—*Africa/Brass*, Impulse!
    Impressions, Impulse!
    My Favorite Things, Atlantic
1962—*Ballads*, Impulse!
    Coltrane, Impulse!
    Coltrane Plays the Blues, Atlantic
    Duke Ellington and John Coltrane, Impulse!
    John Coltrane & Johnny Hartman, Impulse!

1963—*Live at Birdland*, Impulse!
1964—*Coltrane's Sound*, Atlantic
     A Love Supreme, Impulse!

Bibliography

Carno, Zita. "The Style of John Coltrane." *Jazz Review*. November, 1959.

Dargenpierre, Jean-Claude. "John Coltrane: Un Faust Moderne." *Jazz Magazine*. January 1962.

Davis, Miles with Quincy Troupe. *Miles: The Autobiography*. New York: Simon and Schuster, 1989.

DeMichael, Don. "Coltrane on Coltrane." *Down Beat*. September 29, 1960.

Grime, Kitty. "John Coltrane Talks to *Jazz News*." *Jazz News*. December 27, 1961.

Hennessey. *Melody Maker*. August 14, 1965.

Kalbacher, Gene. "Tenor Saxophonist Ravi Coltrane Respectfully Sidesteps the Shadow of a Titan." *Hot House*. November 1995.

Kofsky, Frank. "John Coltrane: An Interview." *Jazz and Pop*. September 1967.

Palmer, Robert. "Alice Coltrane's First Concerts Here in 7 Years." *New York Times*. September 21, 1984.

Porter, Lewis. *John Coltrane: His Life and Music.*Ann Arbor:Th eUniversity of Michigan Press, 1998.

Steadman, Tom. "Coltrane." *Greensboro News and Necord*. September 22, 1991.

Thomas, J. C. *Chasin' the Trane*. New York: Da Capo Press, Inc., 1975.

————. "Trane on the Track." *Down Beat*.October 16, 1958.

Sources

CHAPTER 1: A Jazz Genius

p. 10, "We seemed to attract the most politically advanced blacks..." J.C. Thomas, *Chasin' the Trane* (New York:Da Capo Press, Inc., 1975), 169.

p. 13, "My mother, she was very religious . . ." Lewis Porter, *John Coltrane: His Life and Music* (Ann Arbor: The University of Michigan Press, 1998), 11.

p. 14, "basically a good child, but he was. . ." Ibid., 15.

p. 14, " a very neat child . . ." Ibid., 15.

p. 15, "We'd have hominy grits . . ." Thomas, *Chasin' the Trane*, 4.

p. 17, "We had them all that time and then . . ." Porter, *His Life and Music*, 16-17.

p. 17, "Our mothers had to go to work . . ." Ibid., 19-20.

p. 18, "If the white schools got new books one year . . . " Ibid., 19.

p. 19, "Have you been learning on the side?" Thomas, *Chasin' the Trane*, 17.

p. 20, "I remember John being a very fine little boy . . ." Tom Steadman, "Coltrane,"*(Greensboro News & Record,* September 22, 1991): F5.

p. 20, "He would sit at the (dining room) table and practice . . ." Porter, *His Life and Music*, 33.

p. 22, "For a while, I don't think he had anything but that horn," Ibid., 17.

p. 23, "He didn't like to go down [South] and play . . ." Ibid., 19.

CHAPTER 2: A Young Man in the Big City

p. 27, "We never looked at John as a genius . . ." Porter, *His Life and Music*, 34.

p. 28, "short, squat guy in a pinstripe suit . . ." Thomas, *Chasin' the Trane*, 36.

p. 28, "Well, young man, you are not a chicken . . ." Ibid., 37.

p. 33, "Look, Johnny, I'll buy you a tenor . . ." Ibid., 38-39.

CHAPTER 3: Touring with Dizzy

p. 38, "We don't serve niggers." Thomas, *Chasin' the Trane*, 48-49.

p. 38, "Dizzy was a great teacher and giver . . ." Porter, *His Life and Music*, 79.

p. 40, "He was a very soft spoken . . ." Ibid., 86.

p. 41, "Coltrane would be sitting . . ." Thomas, *Chasin' the Trane*, 66.

p. 42, "How do you know that?" Ibid., 70.

CHAPTER 4: Touring with Miles and Monk

p. 46, "Trane liked to ask all these questions . . ." Miles Davis, with Quincy Troupe, *Miles: The Autobiography.* (New York: Simon and Schuster, 1989), 195.

p. 47, "Miles is a strange guy . . ." Porter, *His Life and Times*, 100.

p. 47, "blew everybody out of the water . . ." Ibid., 99.

p. 48, "All the things I started to do in 1955 . . ." Don Michael, "Coltrane on Coltrane," *Down Beat* (September 29, 1960): 26-27.

p. 48, "When I first joined Miles in 1955 I had a lot to learn . . ." Kitty Grime, "John Coltrane Talks to *Jazz News*," *Jazz News* (December 27, 1961): 13.

p. 48, "People used to tell me Trane couldn't play . . ." Thomas, *Chasin' the Trane*, 74.

p. 50, "I remember his eyes, huge but not staring . . ." Ibid., 76-77.

p. 50, "He reminded me of a large cherub . . ." Ibid., 78.

p. 51, "He would be in the basement practicing . . ." Porter, *His Life and Music,* 104.

p. 52, "He'd be playing in clothes . . ." Ibid., 104.

p. 52, "Man, it was a drag to see how bad Trane was treating himself." Davis, *Miles*, 207.

p. 52, "I've decided to stop smoking, drinking and taking drugs." Thomas, *Chasin' the Trane*, 82.

p. 53, "During the year 1957, I experienced, by the grace of God . . ." Ibid., 106, from liner notes to *A Love Supreme*.

p. 56, "Trane was getting into different harmonic textures . . ." Ibid., 89.

p. 58, "John usually showed up about an hour before the session . . ." Porter, *His Life and Music*, 125.

p. 59, "What sets Coltrane apart from other tenor players . . ." Zita Carno, "The Style of John Coltrane," *Jazz Review* (November 1959): 17-21.

CHAPTER 5: Giant Steps, Kind of Blue

p. 60, "so thick and complex they were almost flowing . . ." Thomas, *Chasin' the Trane*, 106.

p. 61, "Whatever he did he did all the way . . ." Ibid., 104.

p. 61, "epileptic fits of passion." Porter, *His Life and Music*, 139.

p. 62, "If it is interpreted as angry, it is taken wrong." "Trane on the Track," *Down Beat,* (October, 16, 1958): 139.

p. 63, "*So What* is a simple figure based on 16 measures . . ." Bill Evans, from liner notes to *Kind of Blue*, Columbia Records, 1959.

p. 64, "The music has gotten thick." Robert Palmer, from liner notes to *Kind of Blue* 1997 reissue by Sony Music Entertainment Inc., 11. Original Miles Davis quote taken from 1958 interview in *Jazz Review*.

p. 65, "that knocked the jazz world on its ear." Ibid., 145.

p. 67, "I had to separate the musician from the man . . ." Thomas, *Chasin' the Trane*, 119.

p. 68, "That first night Elvin was in the band . . ." Ibid., 130.

p. 68, "I looked at the speedometer and Elvin was doing 90 . . ." Ibid., 132.

p. 69, "The car was a total wreck . . ." Ibid., 132.

p. 70, "I've found you've got to look back . . ." *Down Beat* (September 29, 1960): 131-132.

p. 71, "But, on the other hand, it makes me aware . . ." Jean-Claude Dargenpierre, "John Coltrane: Un Faust Moderne," *Jazz Magazine* (January 1962): 21-25.

CHAPTER 6: Chasin' the Trane

p. 76, "Coltrane may be searching for a new avenue . . ." Porter, *His Life and Music*, 196.

p. 78, "Duke, what do you think?" Thomas, *Chasin' the Trane*, 154-5.

p. 80, "He didn't offer any explanation . . ." Ibid., 166.

p. 82, "Well, these young musicians have to start someplace . . ." Ibid., 169

p. 82, "John Coltrane was more mystic than musician . . ." Ibid., 172.

CHAPTER 7: It Ended All Too Soon

p. 84, "When some evenings, in beginning to play, we feel inspired ..." Porter, *His Life and Music*, 229.

p. 84, "I entered into a phase which was contradictory to the pledge . . ." John Coltrane, liner notes to *A Love Supreme*.

p. 85, "He was talking about death in a philosophical way . . ." Thomas, *Chasin' the Trane*, 186.

p. 85, "When someone is seeing God, that means he's going to die." Ibid., 186-187.

p. 85, "We were both traveling in a particular spiritual direction . . ." Ibid., 172.

p. 86, "He researched, he investigated all the musics of the world . . ." Porter, *His Life and Music*, 274.

p. 88, "I was much disturbed by his music . . ." Thomas, *Chasin' the Trane*, 199-200.

p. 88, "Those who walked out on him in Philadelphia . . ." Frances Davis, "Take the Coltrane," *Village Voice* (February 18, 1992): 74.

p. 89, "When he became avant garde, as they termed it . . ." Porter, *His Life and Music*, 275.

p. 89, "Whenever I make a change . . ." Hennessey, *Melody Maker* (August 14, 1965).

p. 90, "Someone in the audience would stand up," Robert Palmer, "Alice Coltrane's First Concerts Here in 7 Years," *New York Times* (September 21, 1984).

p. 91, "He said he wasn't feeling well," Thomas, *Chasin' the Trane*, 214.

p. 91, "I'm used to the critics complaining about me," Ibid., 203.

p. 92, "It helps me stay alive sometimes . . ." Frank Kofsky, "John Coltrane: An interview," *Jazz and Pop* (September 1967): 23-31.

p. 93, "Coltrane's death shocked everyone, took everyone by surprise." Davis, *Miles*, 285.

p. 94, "When I discovered jazz, I discovered it on my own." Gene Kalbacher, "Tenor Saxophonist Ravi Coltrane Respectfully Sidesteps the Shadow of a Titan," *Hot House* (November 1995): 22.

p. 96, "In this way, I am sharing John's life with the children," Porter, *His Life and Music*, 299.

Websites

Saint John Coltrane African Orthodox Church
www.saintjohncoltrane.org

John Coltrane Festival
www.johncoltrane.com

Wildplace: John Coltrane
http://home.att.net/~dawild/john_coltrane.htm

Index

Wein, George, 90
William Penn High School, 19
WWII, 24, 29, 89

Yokely, Grace, 20
Young, David, 20
Young, Lester, 20, *21*